CREATOR OF ALL

A devotional for kids emphasizing how God created and loves ALL His creation.

By Dr. Anita A. Azeem

Dove Christian
Publishers

Dove Christian Publishers
A Division of Kingdom Christian Enterprises
PO Box 611
Bladensburg, MD 20710-0611

Paperback ISBN 978-1-957497-60-0

Published in the United States of America

Dedicated

To my son Aryeh Azeem, who is fearfully and wonderfully made. Aryeh was born with one extra chromosome that makes him different, but there is such beauty in diversity, as Aryeh has shown our family.

contents

NOTE TO PARENTS

First of all, I would like to congratulate you on opening this book. For some of you, this may be because you're curious about what's inside, and for others, it could be because you genuinely desire to address these topics in front of your young ones. Being a parent of two gorgeous children myself, I know how hard it can be to find just the right book to discuss sensitive issues. For our family, this happens right before bedtime, and so our preference is to find something that is relevant, accurate, Bible-based, short, and clear in communication. Those are the same factors that I kept in mind while writing this devotional. This book is something I would gladly read to my children, and therefore, I hope that it will be beneficial to you as well.

The specific reason for writing on this topic is that as our young children develop, their curious minds start to fill up with countless questions regarding individual differences. They may start asking questions about anyone different from them—a different skin color, belief, gender, or ability. They often begin to wonder about the hierarchy within these categories (who is better than the other). For instance, they may ask whether one skin color is superior to the other. My daughter was only three years old when she first asked me why her skin color was different from that of her friends. We were living in New Zealand, and she was attending Montessori at that time. Kids at the Montessori likely got into a conversation about skin color because they were curious about what such differences meant. Similarly, young children from around the world may begin discussing these issues with their peers early in their lives. They may also be picking up cues from TV shows, books, or the Internet. All this is happening since the child's mind and cognitive abilities are increasing, and they are becoming more inquisitive about the world. Often, parents find it challenging to address these delicate issues and may be unsure of what to say. Some parents try to avoid discussion on these topics due to a lack of trust in their ability to handle these queries.

With this devotional, I aim to help you answer some of the "Why" questions. For instance, why did God create people to be so different from each other? Was it a mistake or an error on His part, or did He intend to create diversity? Also, what does the Bible say about social hierarchies? Did God create one group to dominate the others? I hope that you will find answers and explanations to most of these queries as you read on.

In this book, I aim to highlight the diversity evident in the Bible, explore the need for diversity, and delve deeper into understanding what God says about diversity in His Word.

Welcome to an exciting journey as you begin this Bible-based devotional with your young child, which will provide insight into what God says about differences.

I hope you enjoy reading this devotional with your little one/s.

With Love,

Dr. Anita A. Azeem

STARTING FROM THE CREATION

DIVERSITY is a word that many grown-ups use. It describes how people differ from one another. Some examples include different skin colors, ages, heights, clothing styles, or beliefs. Often, we are scared or unsure about other people who look different or talk differently. This book talks about these differences and explains how God loves everyone.

As we begin reading the Bible in Genesis, which recounts how God created the world, our first clue about diversity can be found in the very first chapter.

In Genesis 1:24, it is written:

"And God said, 'Let the land produce living creatures according to their kinds: the livestock, the creatures that move along the ground, and the wild animals, each according to its kind.'"

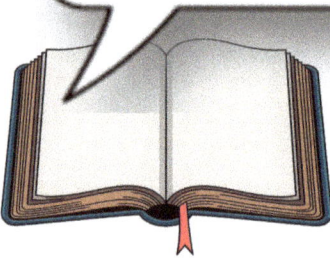

Why did God have to create land creatures, sea creatures, and then those in the sky? And why not just one type to inhabit each? In fact, he made countless types of them. He wanted the earth, the water, and the sky to be filled with animals

that would be distinct from each other. God himself created a world that would be diverse.

He could have just created the same or at least similar types of animals; after all, He is able to do so. However, He purposefully created different kinds of creatures to inhabit the earth. It was His divine plan and purpose for the world to be filled with varying types of animals, all of whom testify to the greatness of the Creator.

How many times have you looked around and seen beautiful patterns of flowers, fruits, insects, animals, or sea creatures? Isn't it amazing how many different patterns there are and how each one is both unique and beautiful? It was all a part of God's plan and purpose. As it says in the scripture, God saw it and said that it was good. He liked the diversity; He made it that way!

Similarly, the world we live in is also

inhabited by people of different kinds. Those with light skin color and those with darker

skin color. Those who are tall and those who are short. Those who speak English and those who don't speak at all. Everyone is precious in God's sight, as He created everyone. It is written in Jeremiah 1:5: "Before I formed you in the womb I knew you, before you were born I set you apart; I appointed you as a prophet to the nations."

He alone formed everyone, and He did so with great purpose. God makes no mistakes,

and therefore, this diverse world in which we live is also there for a purpose. It is all a part of God's perfect plan.

PRAYER:

Dear Lord, help me to understand people who are different from me. Help me to be kind to them and to know that you are the Creator of all. Amen.

PURPOSE OF DIVERSITY

As we begin looking at God's diverse creation, it is important to discuss why he created them like this. Just remember that God does not make any mistakes, and He didn't just accidentally create all these different creatures. He is God: all-knowing, all-powerful, and all-wonderful. He created a world like this for a strong reason.

It was God's divine purpose that the things He created would help one another to create a balance. This is called an *ecosystem*. The

National Geographic Society describes the term *ecosystem* as "a geographic area where plants, animals, and other living things, as well as weather and landscapes, **work together** to form a bubble of life." The keywords are "*work together*." God created an intricate and beautiful system in which plants, animals, and other living things play their part in sustaining the balance of life on Earth.

Nothing that God created was accidental. Even the tiniest of all microorganisms (teeny-tiny living things that can only be viewed with the help of a microscope) have a purpose. They help the world because they help generate oxygen, carbon dioxide, nitrogen, and sulfur. They also help us to digest our food so that we can gain nourishment from it. Most importantly, they help dead plants and animals break apart and rot, and without them, our earth would be covered with dead things all around.

Now, consider all the different plants that God created. Each of them has a purpose. Most of them are helpful as a source of food and nutrition for us. So, if there were no plants, you would have no fruits or vegetables. Think also about the many types of plants and vegetables available to us; each has unique things that help you grow strong and stay healthy, and they all provide different minerals and vitamins to us. That explains why

God didn't just create all fruit to be bananas!

All plants, even those that do not bear fruit, are essential for us as they provide clean breathing air. They absorb carbon dioxide and convert it into oxygen, which is necessary for us to live. God created everything with great care and precision to play a part in the overall balance of the world. Everything and everyone has a purpose, including you!

PRAYER:

Dear Lord, please help me learn to appreciate all of your creations. Even

when I get annoyed with bugs and flies, help me to understand that they, too, were created for a purpose and are a part of your grand plan for the world. Help me see the beauty and focus on goodness in the world.
Amen.

MAN AND WOMAN

On Day 6, God created man, a very unique creature, in HIS OWN IMAGE. This was unlike any of His other creations.

"So God created mankind in his own image, in the image of God he created them; male and female he created them" (Genesis 1:27).

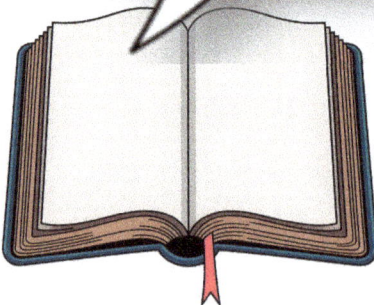

This verse also states that He created them male and female.

In Genesis 2:18, when God saw that Adam was lonely,

"The Lord God said, 'It is not good for the man to be alone. I will make a helper suitable for him.'"

God could have made that helper a copy of Adam, someone completely like him, just like identical twins. However, God thought it was appropriate to create a different helper—oh, how special! Adam would need to understand this helper, someone who did not have the same type of body or the same qualities. God wanted Adam to have a partner who was different from him. Yet this partner, Eve, was also created in God's image. Just a different set of qualities, but still a reflection of God's image.

In this way, God created a friend for Adam who would be more similar to him than any of the other creatures, yet unique in that she wasn't exactly like Adam. God wanted both Adam and Eve to spend time with Him in the

Garden of Eden. He longed for their fellowship and looked forward to spending time with them, and so did they. However, when they disobeyed God, Adam and Eve started to hide from Him, as they were afraid to face Him. Because Adam and Eve did not obey God, they were led away from God. Even today, it is sin (thinking about or doing things that God does not approve of) that leads us away from our wonderful Creator. We ALL need His forgiveness in our lives, whether it is because of lying, stealing, being mean to our siblings, or disobeying our parents—everyone has sinned and falls short of God's glory. BUT He is merciful and quick to forgive us ALL.

PRAYER:

Dear Lord, please give me the courage to seek forgiveness for my sins. Help me to stay strong in Jesus and resist sin that comes from Satan. Amen.

NOAH'S ARK

The next clue about diversity can be found in Noah's Ark.

God told Noah in great detail that:

"You are to bring into the ark two of all living creatures, male and female, to keep them alive with you. Two of every kind of bird, of every kind of animal and of every kind of creature that moves along the ground will come to you to be kept alive. You are to take every kind of food that is to be eaten and store it away as food for you and for them." (Genesis 6:19-21).

It also says at the beginning of the same chapter that God decided He would destroy humans. In fact, in Genesis 6:7, it is written that:

"I will wipe from the face of the earth the human race I have created—and with them the animals, the birds and the creatures that move along the ground—for I regret that I have made them."

God regretted creating humans and decided he would wipe them out, along with all the animals. This would have been a perfect opportunity to get rid of the diverse creatures as well. He was restarting life on Earth and could choose to do it differently this time. Perhaps cut down on the diversity or eliminate some species of animals or birds. What did God do?

He asked Noah to take along two of every kind of bird and land creature and to ensure that there was enough food for them. What?? God wants to create a new world with all the diverse animals, birds, and insects? He also wanted to preserve Noah's sons and their wives so that they could multiply and fill the earth with diverse humans again.

Even though God was upset and regretted creating the world because of the sins of humans, he did want it to stay. He wanted humans to multiply and fill the earth. He also wanted the animals, insects, birds, and fish to survive and multiply, each to their own kind. He liked the diversity in His creation and did not want that to end. Therefore, even in the new world, he included all of the diverse creatures. God likes diversity and did not want to remove that from the world.

PRAYER:

Dear Lord, Thank you for all the lovely animals you have created and the wonderful way in which we all live on earth. Help me to be kind and respectful towards ALL of your creations. Amen.

FOREIGNERS WELCOME IN THE EXODUS

The second book of the Bible, Exodus, also paints a beautiful picture of inclusion. This book talks about the Israelites, the future family of Abraham to whom God promised a new land of their own. At this time, they were the Egyptians' slaves. Then, God sent Moses on a mission to lead the Israelites (God's chosen people) into the Promised Land.

Read Exodus Chapter 9-13 to learn about the story of how God used Moses to speak to Pharaoh and about the ten plagues that came upon the Egyptians. The last one of those was the killing of each family's firstborn male. However, this would not happen to the Israelites if they participated in the Passover. This meant that God gave the Israelites very specific instructions regarding how to avoid losing their firstborn son. God told them to get a lamb (one for each household), take care of it, and on the 14th day, offer it as a sacrifice to God. Then, they were asked to apply the animal's blood to the sides and top of their door frames. That same night, they were also given specific instructions on how to eat the lamb. God told the Israelites that an angel of death would

pass through the land and take away the life of every firstborn in the land. Only those who had the blood of the lamb on their doors would be spared.

Many researchers and Bible scholars have compared the blood of the lamb and the blood of Jesus. This blood at the door protected the Israelites' firstborns from death. Similarly, for those of us who believe in His sacrifice and accept it with our whole hearts, Jesus' blood protects us from spiritual death and destruction.

The important thing to note here is that God allowed foreigners to participate in the Passover if they believed in Him. According to Exodus 12:48:

"A foreigner residing among you who wants to celebrate the Lord's Passover... may take part like one born in the land."

So God extended His mercy towards foreigners as long as they accepted and showed the outward expression of faith.

Similarly, God welcomes all races into His kingdom today if they accept the sacrifice of Jesus on the cross and confess outwardly that they have sinned and fallen short of His glory. Romans 10:9 says:

If you declare with your mouth, 'Jesus is Lord', and believe in your heart that God raised him from the dead, you will be saved..."

This applies to anyone regardless of where they were born or raised. Jesus died for everyone's salvation, and He loves everyone, no exceptions.

PRAYER:

Dear Lord, thank you for sending Jesus for EVERYONE in the world. Help me to show love to other people and help them in whatever way I can. Help me to look past our differences and recognize that your love is for EVERYONE. Amen.

THE RICH AND THE POOR

Often, we measure a person's importance by seeing how famous they are, how much money they have, or the expensive things they own. That is a worldly way of judging people, but that's not how God sees people. In God's kingdom, everyone is important, no matter how much they have or how well-known they are.

Several passages in the Bible make it clear that whether you are rich or poor doesn't matter in God's eyes, and that everyone, regardless of their how much money they have, is welcome into God's kingdom. For example, Proverbs 22:2 says:

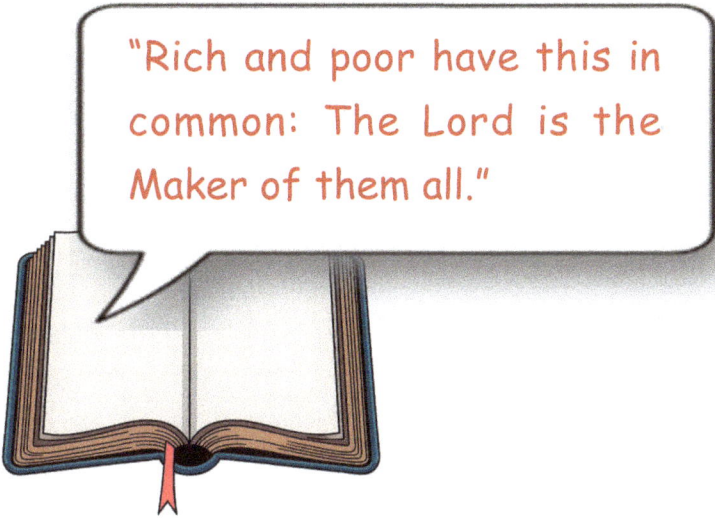

"Rich and poor have this in common: The Lord is the Maker of them all."

This emphasizes that God created everyone, and He is the same for everyone.

God looks at our hearts and not at our possessions, wealth, family, or appearance. 1 Samuel 16:7 says,

"The Lord does not look at the things people look at. People look at the outward appearance, but the Lord looks at the heart."

Similarly, people look at and may care about how big your house is or how fancy your car is, but God does not care about that. He looks at your heart, and if you have invited Jesus to live in your heart, then you've already made the best decision of your life!

James 2:1-7 is another reference in the Bible that warns against treating the poor differently:

"Suppose a man comes into your meeting wearing a gold ring and fine clothes, and a poor man in filthy old clothes also comes in. If you show special attention to the man wearing fine clothes and say, "Here's a good seat for you," but say to the poor man, "You stand there" or "Sit on the floor by my feet," have you not discriminated among yourselves and become judges with evil thoughts?"

Therefore, we should be careful not to focus on outward appearance and riches, as these things do not matter to God. For Him, it is the heart that is more important.

PRAYER:

Dear Lord, thank you for the Bible, which helps us understand Your Word and get to know You in a deeper way. Help me to focus on inward things, such as love, kindness, and compassion, rather than outward things like wealth, possessions, and appearance. Remind me that these things mean nothing to you and that you love everyone the same. Help me to be kind and friendly to everyone. Amen.

YOUNG AND OLD

You might have faced a situation where you were told that you were too old to do something (like being carried in your parents' arms). In some other cases, you may also have heard that you are too young for another set of things (to go camping alone or to drive a car). We have certain standards for what one is able to do or allowed to do at different stages of life. For some activities, it is preferred to be younger, like learning a new language, playing certain sports, or starting ballet; however, for other tasks that require decision-making, greater control, or coordination (like driving a car, voting, or opening a bank account), it's better to be older.

Suppose you are wondering whether Jesus created any distinction between the young and old in terms of who could access him. In that case, I remind you about the time Jesus said,

"Let the little children come to me, and do not hinder them, for the kingdom of heaven belongs to such as these" (Matthew 19:14).

Jesus said this as a response to his disciples who were stopping people from bringing children to Jesus. They assumed that

Jesus had come to the world for adults and would only like to talk to them and teach them. However, Jesus clearly told his disciples off and said that they must let children come to Him, as the kingdom of heaven belongs to such as them.

Jesus is referring to child-like simplicity and faith. Jesus emphasizes that children are important to Him and that He would love to spend time with them.

Another verse that says that both young and old are welcome in God's kingdom is Acts 2:17:

"In the last days, God says, I will pour out my Spirit on all people. Your sons and daughters will prophesy, your young men will see visions, your old men will dream dreams."

This verse demonstrates that God will pour out His Spirit upon individuals regardless of their age. The young will see visions while the old will dream dreams, but God will make Himself known across all ages.

Sometimes, we fail to realize that in God's kingdom, each individual has a unique purpose and calling. We assume that God prefers one group over the other, but that is not true.

PRAYER

Dear God, please help me always remember that everyone is unique and special to you, whether it is my grandparents, parents, or any other adults, myself, or my younger siblings and cousins. Help me appreciate that everyone is welcome in your kingdom, regardless of their age. Amen.

WOMEN AND JESUS

Throughout His life on earth, Jesus refused to treat women as inferior. In those days, the Jewish way of life portrayed men as more

important than women. Men were discouraged from greeting women in public or treating them as important. Women were only allowed to visit the outer courts of the temple, and many Jewish men prayed that they were grateful that they were not born as women. The religious teachings of that time also emphasized that men were superior to women.

Jesus challenged these teachings and rules regarding the treatment of women during his time on Earth. He publicly spoke to several

women. In fact, in Luke chapter 13, we read that Jesus healed a woman who had been suffering for eighteen years. Luke 13:12-13: *"When Jesus saw her, he called her forward* and said to her, 'Woman, you are set free from your infirmity.' Then he put his hands on her, and immediately she straightened up and praised God." Jesus also cured many other women who were sick and needed healing, thereby demonstrating that He had come to Earth to heal men and women. The healing and freedom from sin were for everyone, not just for the men.

Some of the women on whom Jesus performed miracles
- Mary Magdalene (Luke 8:2)
- the woman with the issue of blood (Mark 5:27-34)
- Peter's mother-in-law (Luke 4:38-41)
- Jairus' daughter (Mark 5 and Luke 8)

In Luke 13, Jesus called a woman a "daughter of Abraham." We do not find this term anywhere else in the Bible. Likely, using this term was not something people would usually say. However, Jesus used

it because he wanted to demonstrate that women were equally important in God's eyes.

Jesus not only spoke to several women publicly, but he also healed them and preached directly to them. In the familiar story of Mary and Martha, we see that Jesus encouraged them to sit with Him and listen to His words.

"...Mary, who sat at the Lord's feet listening to what he said." (Luke 10:39)

This was likely the place where men would normally sit. But Jesus knew that what He was saying was important for both men and women, and He told Martha that her sister Mary had chosen the good part.

After His resurrection, Jesus first

appeared to the women who were visiting His tomb. The gospels of Matthew, Luke, and Mark all mention the sequence of events that took place and how Jesus told the women to tell His disciples that He had risen from the dead. Matthew 28:10: "...*Go and tell my brothers to go to Galilee; there they will see me.*" Jesus asked women to spread the good news.

Even today, Jesus calls men and women to reach out to others around them and tell them the good news of salvation.

PRAYER

Thank you for the Bible that tells us how Jesus treated women. Help us to follow Jesus' footsteps and treat everyone with respect and honor. Amen.

THE SAMARITAN WOMAN

In the previous chapter, we discussed how Jesus welcomed women. He spoke to them publicly, extended a healing hand towards them, and even asked them to be His messengers of the good news that He had risen from the dead. In this chapter, we will focus on one interaction that Jesus had with a Samaritan woman, as written in the Gospel of John, chapter 4.

There are a few reasons why this meeting

was so special. First, it is the longest recorded interaction between Jesus and another person in any of the gospels. Next, as discussed in the previous chapter, it was unusual for men to speak to women publicly. Further, this specific woman was a Samaritan, a foreigner. Jews and Samaritans did not get along, and it was strange that a Jewish man would be asking a Samaritan woman for a drink.

Finally, the woman at the well was also living a sinful life. Despite all these differences, Jesus started talking with her. He revealed Himself to her as well and told her that He was the Messiah. Naturally, she was surprised at this revelation, but as we read further, we see that she tells others about Jesus. This was such an important task, and she was chosen for it. In doing so, Jesus broke down all the boundaries of gender, ethnicity, and piety.

In fact, John 4:27 mentions that when Jesus' disciples came back, they were in for a surprise:

"Just then his disciples returned and were surprised to find him talking with a woman. But no one asked, 'What do you want?' or 'Why are you talking with her?'"

John mentioned that they did not ask those questions, implying that those would have been appropriate questions to ask at that time.

Through Jesus' interaction with the Samaritan woman, we learn that He treats everyone with respect, regardless of their identity, social status, ethnic background, or past life. He wanted the message about the arrival of the Messiah to be shared with women, Samaritans, and sinners—everyone!

PRAYER

Dear God, help me never resist talking to other people because they look different or have a different lifestyle. Help me to show your love to everyone. Amen.

SINNERS ARE WELCOME

In the New Testament, Jesus repeatedly reaches out to those who are considered unclean, unholy, unworthy, and generally outcast. In this chapter, we will examine an instance in which Jesus made an effort to communicate with someone who was different and generally not accepted.

Zacchaeus was a short man. He was a tax collector and, therefore, was wealthy according to the scriptures, but the people did not like him. In Luke 19:7, we read that

"All the people saw this and began to mutter, 'He has gone to be the guest of a sinner.'" Zacchaeus had cheated several people, earning himself a bad reputation. However, Jesus decided to go to his house and bless him.

Similarly, Jesus is willing to accept anyone who comes looking for Him and desires to have fellowship with Him. What's also important is that meeting Jesus changed Zacchaeus'

life, as he decided to give away half of his possessions to the poor and return four times the money to anyone he had cheated. Zacchaeus' life changed when he met Jesus. Our lives also change when we invite Jesus into our hearts.

Jesus welcomes all as they are to His throne. But he does want you to leave your sinful ways behind and follow him, just as Zacchaeus did. Jesus said in Luke 19:9-10:

"Today, salvation has come to this house, because this man, too, is a son of Abraham. For the Son of Man came to seek and to save the lost."

Therefore, Jesus invites you as you are. That invitation is for everyone, regardless of age, gender, skin color, or any other characteristic. Jesus wants you to follow Him and give up your sinful ways.

PRAYER

Thank you, Jesus, for inviting us all as we are to come to your throne and have the chance to meet you. Help us to understand your word, grow in it, and flee from everything sinful. Help us lead a Godly life. Amen.

11

Gentiles As Well

We briefly looked at the inclusion of Gentiles (people who are not Jews) when we discussed the Samaritan woman and Jesus' interaction with her. The Bible provides more evidence regarding non-Jewish individuals to show that they are welcomed into the kingdom of God.

While most of this mention is in the New Testament, the earliest passage that talks about all nations is Genesis 26:4:

"I will make your descendants as numerous as the stars in the sky and will give them all these lands, and through your offspring all nations on earth will be blessed."

God is telling Abraham that all nations on earth will be blessed through his offspring. We see a reference to this phrase in Galatians 3:7-8 regarding descendants of Abraham:

"Understand, then, that those who have faith are children of Abraham. Scripture foresaw that God would justify the Gentiles by faith, and announced the gospel in advance to Abraham: 'All nations will be blessed through you.'"

So those who rely on faith are blessed along with Abraham, the man of faith.

This tells us that God had always intended that the Gentiles be included in receiving the blessings. In 1 Corinthians 12, Paul uses the example of the human body to illustrate the diversity within the body of Christ.

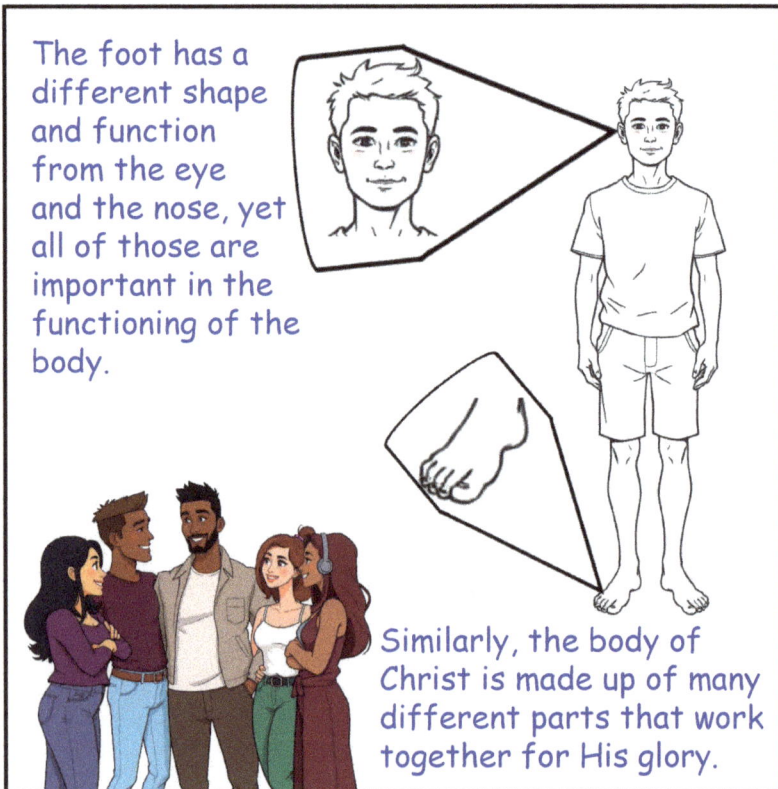

The foot has a different shape and function from the eye and the nose, yet all of those are important in the functioning of the body.

Similarly, the body of Christ is made up of many different parts that work together for His glory.

The apostle Paul is known as the "Minister to the Gentiles," and he worshiped God with individuals from different nations. In several letters, Paul mentions how he was called to the Gentiles and how they were welcomed into God's kingdom. In Romans 1:6:

"And you also are among those Gentiles who are called to belong to Jesus Christ."

We also notice in Acts 13:1-2 that the leaders of Antioch's church included several names of non-Jewish individuals, thereby emphasizing that Gentiles were welcome to accept Jesus and also be part of the Church leadership. This helps us understand that Jesus' sacrifice was not just for the Jews but for anyone who accepts it.

If Jesus did not discriminate in who he

laid down His life for, then why do we fall prey to discrimination? Why do we think that some people are better or more deserving than others?

PRAYER

Dear God, please help me see beyond people's skin color, wealth, and other such things. Help me to be more like Jesus, who did not discriminate. Help me show Jesus' love to everybody. Amen.

one in christ

Jesus came to Earth to connect us and unite us with God. Sin had created a chasm (a great divide) between humans and God,

but Jesus died on the cross, and that cross became a bridge connecting us and leading us back to God.

However, the most important thing to remember about this sacrifice is that Jesus died for everyone. As we read in the previous chapters, He views the rich and the poor as the same. In His sight, adults are no more important than children, nor are Jews more important than the Gentiles. His sacrifice on the cross was to break down all barriers and bring peace on Earth. It is written in Ephesians 2:14-16:

> "For he himself is our peace, who has made the two groups one and has destroyed the barrier, the dividing wall of hostility, by setting aside in his flesh the law with its commands and regulations. His purpose was to create in himself one new humanity out of the two, thus making peace, and in one body to reconcile both of them to God through the cross, by which he put to death their hostility."

If we believe in Jesus' sacrifice, then we should also acknowledge the intention behind it. Further, Galatians 3:26-28 says:

> "So in Christ Jesus you are all children of God through faith, for all of you who were baptized into Christ have clothed yourselves with Christ. There is neither Jew nor Gentile, neither slave nor free, nor is there male and female, for you are all one in Christ Jesus."

The world may be concerned about what your nationality is, how rich you are, or whether you're a boy or a girl, but the Bible tells us that Jesus is the Savior of ALL. It further tells us that we are all the same in God's eyes. He does not care about where we were born or how much money we have. We are all one; there are no barriers dividing us. None of us is preferred over the other in God's sight. We are all the same, and therefore, we should love others just like we love ourselves. This is a hard task, but that's what Jesus asks you to do. In Mark 12:30-31, Jesus sums up the two greatest commandments:

"Love the Lord your God with all your heart and with all your soul and with all your mind and with all your strength.' The second is this: 'Love your neighbor as yourself.' There is no commandment greater than these."

PRAYER:

Dear God, please help me to remember that you do not favor some people over others. When I think I deserve more than others, please help me to realize that you have no favorites and everyone is equal in your sight. Help me to be kind and loving towards everyone. Amen.

13

IN THE END

From the beginning of the first chapter in the first book of the Bible (Genesis) till the very last book of the Bible (Revelation), God's purpose has been clearly revealed. He intentionally, wonderfully, and purposefully created all the creatures as well as Adam and Eve. We noted that throughout the Bible, God shows how He is the maker of all—not just a few, but ALL.

Finally, in the book of Revelation, written by the apostle John, which discusses future events, God reveals to His dear apostle what will happen in the days to come, and he records it for all of us to understand. Revelation is often considered the most complicated book of the Bible, but that's simply because it talks about things that have not yet taken place, so it can be hard for us to imagine things that we have not yet seen.

The book itself talks about several events that will take place in the future. The one that I would like to bring to your attention is Revelation 7:9:

"After this I looked, and there before me was a great multitude that no one could count, from every nation, tribe, people and language, standing before the throne and before the Lamb. They were wearing white robes and were holding palm branches in their hands."

Notice that the verse describes people on God's throne. The multitude consists of individuals from every nation, tribe, people, and language. All these diverse people are gathered before God's throne, praising Him.

They are close to the Creator. Nothing is separating them from God or each other. There is no distinction or rank order based on nationality, color, caste, or language. They are all wearing white robes, which shows they are all equal in His sight. This passage makes it clear that God welcomes all to His throne, and they all have the privilege of praising Him and enjoying His divine presence without any discrimination or distinction. All the things we see on earth (skin color, language, rituals, etc.) will no longer be relevant when we are in front of His throne. We will all be together and praise Him as One.

PRAYER:

Thank you, dear Lord, for the Bible, and thank you for revealing the deepest secrets of your kingdom to us. Help us desire to be close to you. Help us not to be distracted by focusing on differences, and help us know that you are the Creator of ALL and that you love everyone the same way. Help us show your love to others around us. Amen.

14

JESUS FOR ALL

At the end of this devotional, I would like to emphasize the most important message: This is the key message of Christianity. Jesus died on the cross for us, and today, everyone who believes in him shall have eternal life.

"For God so loved the world that he gave his one and only Son, that whoever believes in him shall not perish but have eternal life" (John 3:16).

Jesus was blameless and free of sin, but he took upon himself all the sins of the world. His sacrifice on the cross is for anyone who believes in him.

Romans 10:13 says, "Everyone who calls on the name of the Lord will be saved." Jesus died on the cross for everyone. Revelation 5:9 refers to Jesus redeeming "persons from every tribe and language and people and nation." As we have seen throughout this book, God does not favor one nation, tribe, skin color, gender, or language over the other.

Salvation is a gift from God; it cannot

be earned through good works, charity, or any other means. We can never reach God's standard of purity, no matter how hard we try, but the good news is that salvation is a gift to everyone who accepts it. Jesus has this precious present for you. Will you extend your hands and receive from his goodness?

If you haven't done so already, I encourage you to open your heart and accept Jesus Christ as your Lord and Savior. Understand that the penalty of sin is death, but because Jesus died for our sins, we don't have to. You simply need to invite him to your heart and confess this in front of other people. Here is a prayer for you if you are ready to accept Jesus as your Lord and Savior.

PRAYER:

Jesus, today, I invite you to come into my heart. I accept you as my personal Savior, understanding that it is only through you that I can receive this precious gift. Help me to lead a life that brings many others to you. Help me to grow in the fruits of the spirit: love, joy, peace, patience, kindness, goodness, faithfulness, gentleness, and self-control. Help me to let others know that you died on the cross for everyone and that you love everyone. Help me to extend that love to others as well. Amen.

THOSE WITH SPECIAL NEEDS

In this bonus chapter of the book, I would like to highlight God's love for those who are differently abled. The world often views such people in terms of their limitations, but that's not how God sees them.

Perhaps you know someone who is unable to speak, see, walk, or perform other tasks that most people can do easily. Or maybe you know a 10-year-old who acts like a 3-year-old. You may wonder why God created such people. You may also wonder if Jesus loves them. Perhaps you have noticed someone in your church or in your class at school who becomes easily angered and frequently shouts and runs away. Or maybe it's someone who gets very upset at loud noises or new routines. Perhaps it is a young child in a wheelchair or a 9-year-old who is unable to speak. You may find that to be very odd and sometimes annoying.

I'd like to tie in everything that we have looked at so far in this book in this chapter. Remember how we discussed that God makes no mistakes? Even though some folks might tell you that people with special needs are born because of an error, let me tell you that it is not true. Humans make mistakes; God does not!

In Psalm 139:14, it is written:

"I praise you because I am fearfully and wonderfully made; your works are wonderful, I know that full well."

God has carefully crafted each and every individual—yes, even those with special needs.

While Jesus was on Earth, he reached out to many people who were differently abled.

For example, he healed those who were unable to walk or see, as well as those suffering from leprosy. He did not hesitate to interact with them. He didn't push them away or say that they were mistakes; He reached out to them.

The disciples once asked Jesus if a person was born blind because he had sinned or because his parents had sinned. John 9:2-3: "'Rabbi, who sinned, this man or his parents, that he was born blind?' 'Neither this man nor his parents sinned,' said Jesus, 'but this happened so that the works of God might be displayed in him.'"

God has a plan and a purpose for each person- even those with special needs. Each person is created in God's image, and by showing kindness towards those with special needs, we are showing appreciation for God's creation.

PRAYER:

Jesus, I thank you for those around me who have special needs. Even though I may not be able to understand what they are saying or what they are trying to do, I know that you love them and that they are fearfully and wonderfully created in your image. Help me share this message with my friends. Help us all to be kind to those who are being rejected or bullied because they are different. Give me the courage to be a good friend to them. Amen.

16

MORE ALIKE THAN DIFFERENT

Throughout this book, we have looked at how God does not classify people according to age, wealth, nationality, or ability. To Him, we are all the same, created equally and created in His image.

It is so easy to notice the differences we have with others simply because some of these differences may be too obvious, such as the clothes they are wearing, their skin color, the language they speak, or that they have special needs. Our brains pick up differences very easily.

However, with this final chapter, I want to challenge you to find similarities with people that you meet who look different or speak differently (or don't speak at all). Try to find how you may be more similar than different.

Here's a starting point and some fun facts:

Children from all around the world enjoy playing games. They may have different toys, games rules or ways of doing things but most children enjoy playing games.

Most children also enjoy cold treats like ice-cream on a hot day.

When hurt, most children like to be comforted either by words or actions (like a hug).

So regardless of which country a person was born in, the languages they speak, the food they eat and/or the clothes they wear, we all have the basic need to be loved and cared for.

The Bible verse I'd like to share comes from Proverbs 22:2:

"Rich and poor have this in common: The Lord is the Maker of them all."

This is a great starting point to view that we all have one thing in common: God created us all and in His image to bring glory to His name. Don't shy away from reaching out to someone just because they appear different. Trust me, you will find that they have much more in common with you than you expected, once you get to know them.

Dear God, help me to be able to see your image in every individual I meet. Help me to focus on how they are similar to me and help me to recognize that your love is for everyone. Help me be more like you with each passing day. Help me also to share this very important message with my friends. In Jesus' name.

Amen.

ABOUT THE AUTHOR

Dr. Anita A. Azeem is a social and developmental psychologist who is passionate about nurturing empathy, curiosity, and wonder in children. With a Ph.D. from the University of Otago (New Zealand), her research focuses on reducing prejudice and promoting inclusion through media and storytelling. Dr. Azeem has taught and inspired undergraduate and medical students in three countries—Pakistan, New Zealand, and the United States—and her work has been featured in international journals and

media outlets. *Creator of All* draws from her deep love for faith, diversity, and the shared stories that connect us. Dr. Azeem brings both heart and insight to every page she writes.

She currently teaches at Carson-Newman University and lives with her family in Tennessee, continually inspired by the questions children ask and the wisdom they carry.

www.ingramcontent.com/pod-product-compliance
Lightning Source LLC
Chambersburg PA
CBHW052119030426
42335CB00025B/3060